Introduction To Fiction Writing

For Middle School & High School

Written by:
Stacey Cotrufo

©2011 Stacey Cotrufo

Table of Contents

- Introduction

- Lesson One: Tools for Writing

- Lesson Two: Skeleton Outlines

- Lesson Three: Characters

- Lesson Four: Point of View

- Lesson Five: Setting

- Lesson Six: Formal Outlines & Timelines

- Lesson Seven: Plot Development

- Lesson Eight: Conflict and Resolution

- Lesson Nine: Dialogue

- Lesson Ten: Paragraph/Chapter Structure

- Lesson Eleven: Avoiding Stereotypes & Clichés

©2011 Stacey Cotrufo

INTRODUCTION

Welcome to "Introduction to Fiction Writing"!

Fiction: *a. An imaginative creation or a pretense that does not represent actuality but has been invented.*
b. The act of inventing such a creation or pretense.
2. A lie.
3. A literary work whose content is produced by the imagination and is not necessarily based on fact.
b. The category of literature comprising works of this kind, including novels and short stories.
4. Law; Something untrue that is intentionally represented as true by the narrator.

What does fiction mean to you? If you are a creative writer, then just about everything that you write is fiction; it is made up in your own imagination and not based on any actual event or person.

This workbook is designed to help you, young writers, learn the process of writing a fiction story. There is a process that goes in to writing a good fiction story from idea to completed story and we are going to go over all of them over the next four weeks.

The workshop will cover these lesson topics:
- Outlines and Timelines
- Characters
- Dialogue
- Paragraph/Chapter Structure
- Plot development
- Conflict and Resolution
- Setting
- Point of View
- And so much more!

©2011 Stacey Cotrufo

By the end of this workbook you will have all of the tools you will need to take that story that you have in your head and get it written or typed up and ready for others to read. You'll learn that a good story actually begins before you first type the words "Chapter One". There is a lot of planning that goes in to writing a great story and we want your story to be great! Doesn't that sound exciting?

For today I'll start off with my introduction and give you the posting schedule for the four weeks of our workshop. Also, I would like to go over the expectations for the class so that we are all on the same page as to what you will need to do as participants. I believe that you will get the most out of this workshop if you actively participate in the assignments and discussions. Since we will not all be "in class" at the same time, that gives you, the student, the opportunity to work at your own pace but it also means that you have to hold yourself accountable for getting your work done and assignments in on time.

At the end I'll give all of you a chance to introduce yourselves to the group so that we can get to know each other even though we won't be meeting as a conventional class usually does.

Stacey Cotrufo is a freelance writer from Wake Forest, North Carolina, who is an author or contemporary romance. She self-published her first novel in 2011 went on to release twenty-two books. Her freelance work can be seen on Examiner.com, eHow, Bukisa.com, The Mouse for Less Guest Blog as well as in the Wake Weekly newspaper. She has taught various writing classes to the homeschool community for almost ten years and her classes have included: Creative writing, literary essay writing, research paper writing and more personalized workshops such as dialogue writing and character developing. Stacey is currently writing a contemporary romance and has been an active participant in National Novel Writing Month (NaNoWriMo) and Amazon's Breakthrough Novel Award contests. Most recently, she was a top five finalist in Harlequin's International Editor's Pitch Challenge.

©2011 Stacey Cotrufo

How to Use This Book:

This curriculum was originally designed as a four-week workshop with the lessons posted on Mondays, Wednesdays and Fridays. With the workbook format, you are free to use this as you see fit and spread out the lessons however you want. Each lesson will require some sort of action by you, the student, but most of the assignments will be brief and easy for you to work on. This was how it was done as an on-line format:

Week #1:
Monday - Introduction
Wednesday – Tools for Writing
Friday – Skeleton Outlines

Week #2:
Monday – Characters
Wednesday – Point of View
Friday – Setting

Week #3:
Monday – Formal Outlines & Timelines
Wednesday – Plot Development
Friday – Conflict and Resolution

Week #4:
Monday – Dialogue
Wednesday – Paragraph/Chapter Structure
Friday – Avoiding Stereotypes & Clichés

This is just an example of how to divide up the topics. If you want to use the book five days a week, that will work. If you would only like to use the book once a week, that will work too! Being that creative writing is not usually something done as a primary subject, you fit it in to your schedule wherever you see fit.

©2011 Stacey Cotrufo

TOOLS FOR WRITING

In a perfect world we could all come up with an idea for a story and sit down and write it all out, submit it to a publisher, have them tell us that it is amazing and it would sell a million copies.

Unfortunately, unless you are J.K. Rowling, it doesn't happen that way.

Actually, I am not being very fair to Ms. Rowling because I am sure that there was a lot of work that went in to creating the world that Harry Potter lived in and even if you are not writing a book where you are creating a whole other world, you still have a lot of work to do before you start writing.

We are fortunate that we live in the computer age. Before the creation of the computer, there were typewriters. These were horrible machines (although at the time we thought them amazing) because they did not self-correct, they did not allow you to see what your page would look like before it printed; all in all you had to take a lot of time and go slow or you had to be prepared to continually start over with a fresh sheet of paper.

I think there is something to be said about writing things out by hand and not using a computer but whatever works for you, THAT is what you should use. What do I mean by all of this rambling? It's simple, you can get no further in this class until you decide on that very first tool to use for writing: paper and pen/pencil or computer. Once you know that, the rest will be a breeze…or at least somewhat easier.

As a writer myself, I use a combination of the two. I tend to scribble down lists and notes when I am away from my computer and then go and type them all up so if that works for you, that is fine. Just make a commitment to you major writing tool and we'll go from there.

So after completing that first hurdle, you're probably thinking "What else is there?" You see, it's not only about sitting down and writing. Oh, if only it were that simple! No, in order to make the writing process flow with as few interruptions as possible, it is important for you, the writer to have all of your tools at your disposal so that when inspiration strikes, you will be prepared.

©2011 Stacey Cotrufo

Introduction to Fiction Writing　　　　　　　　　　　Lesson One – page 5

You should have your pad, pen/pencil, computer to start with. Next, you should have a good dictionary and thesaurus at your disposal. This could be the on-line formatted one or the physical books but either way, make sure that you have them close at hand so that if you are just flowing with story ideas you don't have to stop, get up and go searching for a dictionary or thesaurus and then by the time you find one, you've forgotten why you needed it!

Next, find a spot where you are comfortable writing. When I used to teach classes in a classroom, I encouraged my students to get comfortable; take off their shoes, move their chairs, sit on the floor if need be, but you will find that your words will flow easier if you, the writer, are comfortable. Not everyone finds sitting at a desk with a hard chair the best way to write and that's okay! Sit on your bed, sit on the floor, sit on the couch…sit outside if you want to! The point is to not lock yourself in to the thinking that you have to be in a formal position (table/desk and chair) to write.

Okay, we're making some progress now! Those are the basic essentials, now we are going to dig a little deeper. Ready?

Computer Programs:

Are you using Microsoft Word? What edition? Are you using Open Office? Word Pad? The most common program for writing (and submitting) is Microsoft Word which is part of Microsoft Office. The program itself can be a little pricey but it is a good investment to make. With the newer versions you will be able to convert your documents in to a PDF file which seems to be what a lot of publishers are looking for so it's something to consider if you are serious about doing anything with your book once it is completed.

Get familiar with the program that you are going to be using; learn all that you can about it because while you may be excited to just get going and type to your heart's content, the editing process that you will have to go back and do can be time consuming and painful if you have no idea what to do. How does the spacing work, how are headers/footers/page numbers inserted?

I will be honest with you, this is a big deal if you are a serious writer whose ultimate goal is to submit a manuscript to a publisher. I actually took a

©2011 Stacey Cotrufo

month-long online course on formatting a novel in Microsoft Word and let me tell you, it was very eye opening. I thought that I knew enough about the program to do what I had to do, but that workshop opened up a whole new world for me and showed me things that I never knew MS Word could do! There are plenty of places on line where you can go for a tutorial to learn the basics of MS Word and office, but one that I found to be reputable was http://www.gcflearnfree.org/. With this you can choose your version of Microsoft Office and which aspects of it you want to learn.

Books and Other Resources:

This can be relatively simple or complex, depending on what you are writing. One of the most important tools to have at your disposal are books that you enjoy that are similar to what you want to write. If you enjoy science fiction books, read as many of them as you can. Analyze them and see what publishers look for in a story. Look at different writing styles of different authors and take your cues from them.

There was a particular romance publisher that I wanted to write for. There was a very specific division of theirs whose books I loved and knew I could write for. I read all of the books that I could get my hands on and learned, rather quickly, that there was a very distinct formula to all of their stories. It wasn't that they were all exactly alike, per se, but there was definitely enough similarity to the layout of the stories that made it easy to follow.

So first, read as much as you can the genre that you want to write. Next, think about where and when your story is most likely to take place and collect books, brochures, websites – any reference material you can on that place or time period because you will want it readily available to you once you start formatting your outline. Do not wait until you are deeply entrenched in your story to realize that you have no idea what the wardrobe or fashions were like in say, 1927. Having to stop and do that research can take valuable time away from your creative writing moment and believe me, writers block can strike at any time so do whatever it takes to take advantage of the time when the ideas are flowing.

I'm not saying that you should do all of your research right now, but you should have access to all of your reference material at all times during the writing process.

©2011 Stacey Cotrufo

I have a drawer in my desk that is strictly for travel brochures, maps, and whatnot pertaining to places in the country that I have used in my stories. All of my stories are written in the present day so travel brochures work great.

If you use websites for references and research, make sure that you bookmark them ahead of time so that you can just click and be where you want to be to get the information that you want to get.

Another great resource, especially if you are writing anything historical, are movies. I had a student who was writing a story that was set back in the 1930's. In order to really make her story feel authentic, she did a lot of research by watching classic movies that really showed the fashions and the dialogue of that time. If you were writing a story that was set even twenty years ago, you need to be aware of the "lingo" – how people spoke. No one knew what "Tweeted" meant or what Facebook is so having a visual of the time period can be a great resource.

Time

One of the greatest recourses in for your writers toolbox is time. I will not lie to you, writing a novel, no matter how long or short, takes time. In the fast-paced world that we live in, most of us don't have a whole lot of spare time to sit down and write. You have to make the time. You have to commit to finding the time and being productive during that time to work toward your goal.

Every November there is a phenomenon known as NaNoWriMo – otherwise known as National Novel Writing Month - http://www.nanowrimo.org/. You go to the website, you register, you write, you validate your work during the course of the month and the goal is to write 50,000 words in a month. Most of what you write will be horrendous and need some deep editing, but what your goal should be is to WRITE those 50,000 words. No editing, no formatting, just writing. This is a great motivational tool. If you can write that much in a month, than you are off to a great start with your novel. You can go back and edit and format later but they just want you to get the words on the page!

©2011 Stacey Cotrufo

There are no real prizes for competing in this – it is a personal accomplishment. Sure, you get a certificate and they have even given away coupon codes to those who hit the 50,000 word mark to go to CreateSpace (a self-publishing website through Amazon.com) to get a free printed copy of your book. Most of the time, you will get the copy of the book and look at it and think "What was I thinking?" but it's kind of cool to have a printed copy of a book that you wrote with your name on it.

The Most Important Tool

Your imagination.

It sounds corny, I know, but that is the truth. You have to trust in your own imagination and do whatever it takes to feed that and keep the creative ideas coming. It's very easy to read something that someone else has written and go "Great idea!". Let your ideas be the great ones. You don't want to copy someone else's work or their plot/ideas, you need to find a way to make your own and bring those ideas to life.

Not every idea is going to make a great COMPLETE story. In the past I have had some wonderful ideas for a story only to find that I didn't have enough to keep it going for 65,000 words. And you know what? That was okay! You move on to the next idea or you dig a little deeper to see what you can do to enhance/add to the story and make it complete.

Homework:

Okay, so a lot of what we talked about today is not about writing anything, it's about preparing to write. What I want you to do is to make a list of what your writing toolbox is going to look like – where are you comfortable writing, what genre are you writing, where are you finding your resources, what computer program are you using, etc.

If you get your tools lined up and organized, it will go a long way in helping you to focus on what it is that you really want to do – write!

©2011 Stacey Cotrufo

Introduction to Fiction Writing Lesson One – page 9

My Writer's Toolbox

_____

_____

_____

_____

_____

_____

_____

_____

_____

_____

©2011 Stacey Cotrufo

Skeleton Outlines

So you have an idea for a story.

Good for you!

Now you have to write it.

Boooo!!!

Wouldn't it be great if we had a story idea and it just magically found its way to be written out – with perfect formatting and grammar and all of the plot twists done for you??

SO NOT HAPPENING!

Having an outline is a very important part of the early writing process. Just having one doesn't commit you fully to the story, but writing it down, having it on paper, is a great way to document what you're thinking and then you can choose whether or not you are going to actually use that idea now or at a later date. Sometimes, I'll write a basic outline for a story, then life gets in the way, and I can go to my journal of story ideas at a later date and find an outline or story idea that I've written down and use that as a prompt to get me writing.

For this lesson we are going to start with the most basic of outlines. A skeleton one, so to speak. I found a great description of what a good skeleton outline should include and it comes from Scribendi.com:

"Many writers forget that a skeleton is just that—bare bones. Humans all have skeletons that look pretty much alike, but we all look vastly different when flesh, hair, and snazzy clothes cover them up. The plot outline is not the be-all and end-all of your plot; it's just the scaffolding holding up the walls of your construction.

©2011 Stacey Cotrufo

Your outline is just the beginning. Writing one does not carve anything in stone; it is there to help you have a general direction for your story.

Before you start your actual novel outline, spend some time brainstorming freely, letting your imagination run, generating ideas, and writing them down.

Some questions to ask yourself before you take pen to paper (or fingers to keyboard) are:

- Who will be your main character?

- What is this story about?

- Where and when (in general) will your story take place? In Miami in the early 1980's? On the planet Fiz in the year 2044?

- In general, what type of novel are you writing? Is it mainly comedy? Drama? A thriller?

Where do we begin?

The first thing we want to write down is a very general, SHORT version of our story idea. It could be something as simple as : *Four friends spend a final summer together celebrating the bonds of friendship before one of them gets married.*

Or it can get more detailed:

Grace, Julianne, Maggie and Lily spend a final summer together celebrating the bonds of friendship before Lily marries her long-time boyfriend, Joe. It was a time to kick back, relax and have nothing more to do than enjoy one another's company but it turns in to a summer of life-changing proportions when Grace finally admits her feelings for Ethan, Julianne admits to a secret relationship that is bound to anger her parents, Maggie decides to end her five-year relationship with Brian and Lily turns in to a Bridezilla!

©2011 Stacey Cotrufo

Neither of these statements is eloquently written but the basic ideas are the same; the second one is just the expanded version. So don't get caught up in making that basic plot description sound perfect, as time goes on and if you decided to take this story to the next level and pitch it to an editor or agent or publisher, you will rework that "blurb" until you are cross-eyed. You'll fine-tune it until you have it down to the perfect wording. That is not necessary at this point.

Characters are next.

You will do a bare-bones listing of your MAJOR characters. Just their names and a basic description of them physically and maybe a little bit of info in to who they are.

For example: Lily Madison, blonde, blue eyes, age 24. Outgoing, loves her friends and family, super-excited bride. Strong-willed.

As we go on, we will do a much more detailed character description but for the sake of our skeleton outline, this is all of the info that you will need.

Where is your story taking place? If your story is set in present day, all you would need to write is Emerald Isle, North Carolina, present day. But if you are going historical, you'll want the time period that you are writing in or if you are going futuristic, creating your own world/place, you'll want to give those details here, as well.

And finally, what kind of story are you writing? Here is a list of the most common Fiction genres:

- Action Adventure, Crime, Detective, Fantasy, Horror, Mystery, Romance, Science Fiction, Western, Inspirational.

Knowing your genre is an important tool because there is a possibility of not having a good target audience if the genre isn't clearly defined. For example: I do book reviews for several websites. I had stated that my preference for books were contemporary romances. So they sent me one. It was a crime drama/mystery that had some romantic elements.

©2011 Stacey Cotrufo

Believe me when I tell you that that book was in no way, shape or form, a contemporary romance. It was 90% crime drama/mystery and I really do not enjoy that type of story at all. Needless to say I did not have a good review for it.

Know the type of story that you are writing so that you will know who will want to read it.

Homework:

So what's your story idea? Remember, you can write it up in just a sentence or two or in a brief paragraph. Who are your main characters? If your story has a bunch of characters, you don't need to list them here; we want just the main ones. We'll get in to secondary characters and looking at them all more closely in a later lesson. What genre are you writing and when does your story take place?

Write up your outline – it's your first step in getting started!

_____

_____

_____

_____

_____

_____

_____

_____

©2011 Stacey Cotrufo

Introduction to Fiction Writing

Characters

Okay, let me start by saying that this lesson is going to have a LOT of information for you to take in, but by the end of it, when your homework is complete, you are going to have an incredibly REAL character for your story.

All stories have at least two main characters. I'm not saying that every book ever written is that way but basically, two main characters is the norm. For the sake of this lesson, we are only going to focus on ONE character in your story. If you have two main characters, when it comes time to do the homework, please just choose one of them to submit information on and then use the information you learned to create your second character on your own.

So where do we begin? Well, from your skeleton outline, you should have at least a basic idea of who your characters are. Pick one. You should have a general idea of what they look like and a little bit of info in to the kind of person they are. Now we can begin to dig deeper. We're going to start with the easy stuff, the physical stuff, and then really delve in to who they are.

Physical Descriptions: What do they look like?

Brown hair, brown eyes, round face, freckles…sure, that would be an accurate description for some but not every person with brown hair and brown eyes looks the same. There has to be *more.*

Some things to include in a physical description include: Eye color, hair color, skin tone, face shape, height, build and anything that is obvious about someone's appearance. Do they wear glasses? Do they wear a certain type of clothing? Is their hair style something out of the ordinary or do they wear a hat or some sort of hair accessory that makes them easy to identify? Is their hair curly or straight? Do they wear a certain type of jewelry that stands out when you see them? How do they walk?

©2011 Stacey Cotrufo

There is a way to state things that can make it sound more interesting, as well. For example, not everyone with brown hair has plain brown hair. You can use phrases like "rich brown", "mahogany", "chestnut", "light brown", "dark brown", etc. The same can be said with eye color – it's not always cut and dried on what shade of color someone's eyes are. Blue eyes come in many different shades and the more specific you write, the more your reader will be able to clearly picture your character in their minds as they read your stories.

I don't know about you, but I enjoy a story much more if I can clearly picture the characters in my mind.

Who are they? Giving your character a history

We all have a history. We have lived many years, had things happen to us, we've traveled places, we've met people, taken classes, learned different skills…we have life experiences that make us the people that we are today.

No two people, not even twins, share the same history. Yes, within a family you may have similar traits, looks, characteristics; you may have travelled to the same places and learned the same things, but our interactions with people are what truly can shape the people that we are. Being able to identify with some of these things can help you with your character and then help you with your story.

Think about your story. While your story may take place during a very short period of your character's life, there is a reason why they are the person that they are and as the creator of that character, you get to decide exactly what those reasons are! How cool is that?

So thinking about your character, what kind of person are they? Quiet? Outgoing? Bold? Comical? Mean? Selfish? Giving? This is where you get to have fun. You get to create someone essentially since birth. You can describe what sorts of things have happened in their lives, what kind of family they come from. You do not have to make this in to a novel itself. Most of the history that you give them may never be mentioned in your story in any great length, but for YOU the writer to really understand them, you are going to have to create and know what makes these people tick

©2011 Stacey Cotrufo

Some things to think about when writing up your character's history are:
- How old are they?
- Where are they from?
- Do they have siblings?
- How big is their family?
- What are some of their likes and dislikes and why?
- A brief physical description
- Give them at least ONE traumatic incident from their childhood
- Who influences them and why?
- What is their job/career? (if they are an adult)
- What are their hobbies? Talents?
- Give them at least one embarrassing moment
- What is their highest education and what did they study?
- What is their relationship like with their best friend?
- What are they afraid of?
- What makes them happy?

Giving your character a voice:

Here's something funny to think about: Imagine that you are having a conversation with your best friend. You are telling them something exciting that happened to you and they sat facing you, back straight, arms at their side, a blank expression on their face and said in a very monotone voice "That's nice."

It would be a bizarre thing to witness, wouldn't it? That's because whenever we talk to another person, we become fairly animated. No one really sits one hundred percent still, with no facial reaction and no voice inflection while talking to another person. It doesn't matter if the person is right there in front of you or on the phone, we move, we laugh, we smile, we yell, we raise our voices, we whisper…there are hundreds of options as to how we act or react while in conversation with other people.

©2011 Stacey Cotrufo

Does your female character twirl her hair? Does your character stutter? Are they nervous? Do they have any sort of OCD behavior? Do they speak softly or are they loud and boisterous? Are they reserved? Happy? Angry? Are there any patterns of behavior that you want to have for them?

And then there is quite literally their voice. How do they speak? I have a pretty heavy New York accent. Living here in North Carolina, I am surrounded by people with Southern accents. I am a loud talker and a loud laugher. Some people speak quietly and would never be seen just laughing out loud. I have been known to speak my mind (only to those that I am extremely comfortable with) while at other times I keep my opinions to myself and let things stay bottled up.

These kinds of actions are important in a character because if your character is confrontational but somewhere along the line learns to be a little bit more reserved and controlled, that would make for interesting character development. It shows a great contrast and we would see the transformation in your story.

Family Matters:

We all come from somewhere. That's the reality. We all grow up with people around us and whether they are our biological family or not, they affect our lives.

I grew up with a mother, a father and one sister. My parents divorced when I was ten. My dad remarried first; I was seventeen and I gained a step-brother from that marriage. My mom remarried when I was nineteen and I gained three step-brothers and one step sister from that marriage. My once small family was suddenly quite large.

So what kind of family does your character come from? Big or small? Are they the oldest? Youngest? Any traumatic family events? Do they have a good relationship with their parents? With their siblings? Is there a family business that they are a part of or pressure to be a part of one? Are they competitive or laid back?

©2011 Stacey Cotrufo

Introduction to Fiction Writing   Lesson Three – page 18

Homework:

Okay, I'm not going to lie to you; this is a pretty lengthy assignment. That's why I asked you to choose only one of your characters to work on this time.

I want you to look at this as a research paper type of assignment. The main difference is that instead of going to the library or going online to research a famous person or a historical figure, you are researching your main character and most of that research will be done in your own head! You are going to essentially create this person. I am not saying that you have to start at the moment of their birth, but it is important to give them a life because the things that happen to us in life, make us who we are.

All of those topics we covered are there for a reason. We all look different, sound different, act different, respond different. If we were all the same, there would be no need for fiction stories – they would all sound the same. There would be no movies – they'd all end the same.

Go wild with this topic. Create the type of character that make us want to know more about them! Make them the kind of people that we will root for, care about and want to read about. Breathe life in to them. Make them your own.

Like I said, this is going to be lengthy. Don't rush it. Don't feel the need to hand in the assignment first. I would rather have it come in and be submitted in a few days with it being complete than have it come in early and be missing some important details.

Think about the person that you are. What are some significant things that have happened in your life that have made you who you are today? Use yourself for inspiration or someone that you know and admire. The possibilities, again, are endless!!

©2011 Stacey Cotrufo

The Art of Dialogue Writing — Lesson One – page 19

©2011 Stacey Cotrufo

Point of View

Who is telling your story? We know that YOU are writing it but from whose point of view is that story being told?

This is a topic that can exhaust a writer. Think about the books that you currently enjoy reading. Who is telling the story? Is it the main character telling it, using phrases like "I went on a mission" or "I said"? Or is it in the third person where it's a lot of "They did" or "he said"?

Here is a definition of Point of View: The Point of View (POV) determines the narrator of a story and how much the reader knows. Writer use first, second or third person with purpose. First, second and third person Point of View (POV) specify through whose eyes the story is told.

Point of view comes with many different descriptions. We're going to start with the basics and then get a little more in-depth. I was trying to think of the best way to describe this topic and searched the internet for ideas and found some examples that I'd like to share with you. Some of this comes from Leigh Michaels' Classroom on the Web website:

First person: (includes the thoughts and perspective of one main character, who's telling his/her own story)

As I walked up the hill, I realized that the atmosphere was just too quiet. There was no sound from the cardinal who was nearly always singing from the top of the maple tree. I thought I saw a shadow move high up on the slope, but when I looked again it was gone. Still, I shuddered as I felt a silent threat pass over me like a cloud over the sun.

Key Words: I, me

First Person POV is a story told in the narrating character's own voice. It uses "I" throughout, and the reader doesn't know any more than the character does.

©2011 Stacey Cotrufo

Example: I was minding my own business when Mom burst in. "What's with you?" I grumbled.

If the reader is to know that Mom is angry, it must be shown through her words and body language available to the "I" character and not through Mom's thoughts (unless psychic abilities are one of the narrator's traits).

Second person: (turns the reader into the character)

As you walk up the hill, you realize that the atmosphere's just too quiet. There's no sound from the cardinal you know is almost always singing from the top of the maple tree. You think you see a shadow move high up on the slope, but when you look again it's gone. You shudder as you feel a silent threat pass over you. You feel cold, like a cloud just passed over the sun.

Key Words: You

Stories told in second person are told as if telling someone else what they are doing.

Example: You walk into the cave and hear a low rumble. "What is it?" you wonder.

While second person POV is occasionally used in literary stories, and was successful in Jay McInerney's *Bright Lights, Big City*, it is generally considered to distance the reader instead of drawing them into to identify with the character. One of its common uses today is in interactive fiction, such as the "Choose Your Own Adventure" stories.

I'll be honest with you, there are not many books that I have read that are in the second person. I'm sure they are out there and if you have read them and enjoy them, that's great. All I'm saying is that the majority of books that are currently out there aren't written in this particular POV. If you are comfortable with it and want to try it, you should go for it!

©2011 Stacey Cotrufo

Third person: (includes the thoughts and perspective of one character at a time)

As she walked up the hill, she realized that the atmosphere was just too quiet. There was no sound from the cardinal who she so often heard singing from the top of the maple tree. She thought she saw a shadow move high up on the slope, but when she looked again it was gone. Nevertheless, she shuddered as she felt a silent threat pass over her. It felt like a cloud creeping over the sun.

Key Words: She, her, him, he, them

Third person is the familiar he said / she said story.

Example: He gripped the dollar bill tightly. "You can't have it," he told her.

Depending on the author's choice, it can be very limited, pulling the reader into the head of the narrator, or completely omniscient, letting readers see all the characters' thoughts.

I think it is somewhat safe to say that a majority of the fiction books we read are written in the third person. That's not to say that it's not okay to use first or second person, but the most popular point of view to go with is the third person. Essentially, YOU, the writer, are writing the story and telling the story about your characters.

Multiple Points of View

A story with multiple points of view is not the same as omniscient. Multiple viewpoints let the reader into different characters' heads by making complete narrative switches, usually in different sections or chapters. Within those sections, however, the narrator is held to a single, usually limited, viewpoint.

Stories using multiple POVs include:

- *The Hunt for Red October* by Tom Clancy
- *The Memory Keeper's Daughter* by Kim Edwards
- *The Sisterhood of the Traveling Pants* by Ann Brashares

©2011 Stacey Cotrufo

There are several other, more in-depth options that we could look at but considering that this is an introductory class, I have chosen to leave it with those four topics because I think they are easy enough to fit yourself in to.

A lot – if not most – stories that I have read are written in the third person / multiple points of view category. That is saying that in different scenes, we are getting in to different characters heads or sometimes during the same scene we can describe what each character is thinking when the dialogue or subject is directed at them.

Okay, so as of RIGHT NOW, where do you find yourself? How do you write? Have you read books in each of these points of view? Which one do you think would be the easiest to work with?

Homework:

I want you to write four different scenes, each from one of the points of view listed above. So you will have a short scene written in the first person, one in the second, one in the third and one with multiple. You do NOT have to use your characters or even your story. I just want to see that you understand how each is written.

Also, please answer the four questions listed before the homework assignment. The where do you find yourself, how do you write, etc. questions. I'm curious to learn more about your writing styles.

_____

_____

_____

_____

_____

©2011 Stacey Cotrufo

Setting

What exactly does the phrase "setting" mean? One definition lists it as that is where the plot takes action or the environment around it. The setting is the background in terms of time and place. For example, a novel could be set in modern Chicago, in New York City in the 1950s, in Spain in the 1820s or in an imaginary future society.

Another description that I found regarding setting had this to say:

The setting of a novel encompasses a number of different, but linked, elements:

* Time - day or night; summer or winter; the historical period (an actual date)

* Place - inside or outside; country or city; specific town and country; real or fictional

* Social - the minor characters who take little part in advancing the plot, but whose presence contributes to the realism of the novel

* Mood and atmosphere - eerie; dangerous; menacing; tense; threatening; relaxing; nostalgic; happy; light-hearted etc.

I think when we normally thing of a setting of a story, it is the very basics: Time and place. But the more we look at it, the mood, atmosphere and our minor characters play a large role in making for a very interesting setting.

If you were to think about yourself and your life right now, what is your setting? Modern day, North Carolina, home. That is a good description of your setting. But what if we went deeper? Modern day, Wake Forest, North Carolina, dining room of 1945 historic home. Okay, a little more detail (and we always want details!).

©2011 Stacey Cotrufo

And we can even go deeper still. Modern day, Wake Forest, North Carolina, dining room of 1945 historic home, twilight on a stormy September night as I sit at my desk and try to come up with ideas for my next story.

Okay, it's not riveting or anything, but it basically describes the setting of the scene I am living right now. Riveting isn't always the goal but the describing your setting in the right way, will draw your readers in and make them believe and get excited about what it is that you are writing about.

I found this description of setting: *"In your novel, you can control the climate, traffic, parking, and everything else right down to the smallest detail. You can create a perfect world or one that isn't so perfect. It can be a real place, such as your hometown, or one you dream up. In short, it's your world. You are only limited by your imagination and your researching ability."*

So again we wonder, how important is setting? The website "Fiction Factor" says the following:

"Whether your story takes place on an imaginary world or right here on present day earth, setting is a crucial part of any story. How you build the world around your characters will play a vital role in the overall believability of your novel. The type of world you create will determine the reactions and behaviors of your characters. Consider this: a woman's role in society will vary drastically from the 1920's Midwest USA to a 2001 professional woman of a major city to the present day attitudes towards women in a Muslim country. A story set in any of these times should reflect the social mores of that particular culture."

Think about some classic stories (or movies) that you enjoy and think about the setting. First, think about the Harry Potter series. The whole mystical world of Hogwarts is something that made that story so amazing and enchanting. Imagine if you had the same characters, but no magical castle and say the story took place…on a regular, everyday farm in North Dakota. It doesn't work.

©2011 Stacey Cotrufo

What about Star Wars? Again, imagine the same characters and the same basic story line and plot taking place in today's world. It just wouldn't work. Or how about all of those Jane Austen movies? What if they were taking place in their proper time and place but the characters were wearing jeans, sneakers and eating McDonald's? IT DOESN'T WORK!!!

Setting is so much more than the where and when. That is the biggest thing to remember. Every scene you write, you need to set the scene to some extent and keep the story on track. If your story is futuristic, you can create any kind of gadget and if described properly, the reader will believe you – even if such a gadget hasn't been invented yet. But if your piece is tied to a particular period of time, you must do your homework and research what the wardrobe was, the speech, the inventions, etc. to make your story believable.

Homework:

I know this lesson was relatively short but I want each of you to think about your story that you are using for this class. Where is it set? What is the year/time period? I want you to fully explore the basic setting of your book and write it down in paragraph format – JUST THE SETTING, NOT THE CHARACTERS.

Next, I want you to write a scene where the setting plays a huge part – whether it's a character walking through the town you've created or exploring a place that is a key element to your story. Something that will give us a view in to the world you are writing about.

_____

_____

_____

_____

©2011 Stacey Cotrufo

Introduction to Fiction Writing   Lesson Six – page 33

Formal Outlines and Timelines

This is quite possibly my favorite topic and one that, if I could, I would do an extensive and intensive workshop on all by itself. Having said that, brace yourself, it's going to be a long lesson. Actually, this lesson and the two after it are all going to be tied in together.

Okay, so we already have our skeleton outline in place. Everyone should have at least that lesson done. In that skeleton, you have just the basic info – who, what, where, when, etc. Now we are going to take those parts and flesh them out, dig deep and really get in to our stories. We are going to start with the outline and then in the second part of the lesson we will look at making a timeline.

Take out your skeleton outline and see what you have written. There's not much there, right? You have the somewhat difficult task ahead of you of mapping out the story. You may not have thought out all of the details, but you are going to now.

Before we go any further, please, please, PLEASE keep in mind that your work is a work in progress. Anything that you write down right now for the sake of this lesson does not set it in stone! At any point in the writing process you may decide to change something – whether it is just one particular scene or deleting a character or even re-working the entire storyline. That is all okay! You are allowed to do that. I don't want anyone freaking out that they cannot do this lesson because they are not sure exactly where they want their story to go. So please take a deep breath, relax and we'll get started.

I want you to think about the outline as an amazingly helpful tool. The more info you write down now, the easier it will be for you to get in to the writing of your story and have less distractions/writer's block. That's not to say that you won't have those things, but a well-written outline will definitely help you to stay on task.

Let me tell you a little story about an experience that I had and the difference an outline can make. Back in 2009 I had found out, quite by accident, about NaNoWriMo – that is National Novel Writing Month. It is held every November on-line and you have 30 days to write

©2011 Stacey Cotrufo

50,000 words. So from November 1 to November 30, you are encouraged to write, write, write, write, write – not edit, not format, just write. The purpose is to get you in the zone and prove to yourself that you can do this.

There are no great big awards; you do get to print out a certificate but there is no ONE big winner. Everyone who gets to 50,000 words gets the certificate. They have a counter on the site that you can upload your work to and it does the word count and keeps track of it for you. If you've never participated, I highly recommend it.

So anyway, I found out about this phenomenon on October 31st. At 10:00 at night. Luckily I had a story that had been swirling around in my mind so the next morning I sat down to write. And I wrote like a crazy person except for the fact that I had a lot of moments where I had to go BACK and read what I had written because I had forgotten my heroine's last name or what color hair she had. I was forgetting the basics because I never bothered to write it down!

In 2010, I was prepared. The week leading up to NaNoWriMo, I was an outline fiend. I had thorough physical descriptions of all of my characters, I had their personalities all figured out, I knew exactly where my story was going to go from start to finish and I have to tell you, it was a WAY more enjoyable November.

Sure, taking the time to do this, particularly when you have a story in your head that you are dying to get started on, can seem tedious but believe me, it is really well worth it.

Now we are ready to begin…

We are going to be writing this up in paragraphs. Each step, each time we start to write about something new, I want you to start a new paragraph – no block format. No big giant 5-page paragraph. I want you to follow these steps and to double space between your paragraphs for ease in reading.

Your first paragraph is going to be all about your main character. If you have two main character, give them each a paragraph of their own. This is based on your character description from lesson three.

©2011 Stacey Cotrufo

Introduction to Fiction Writing   Lesson Six – page 35

I know in that lesson we only worked on one character but now you will get to work on the other one – if there is one.

Please do not get in to secondary characters yet. They will have a place of their own. For now we are focusing solely on your main characters. So paragraphs one and two should be dedicated to them.

Your next paragraph is sort of your introductory plot paragraph. You are going to give a brief description of your overall story. It should be maybe 5-10 sentences tops.

Your fourth paragraph will start with the story details. Imagine, if you will, that your story is split in to thirds. Your fourth paragraph is about the first third of your story. This is normally where conflict is set up, the story builds, and this is where you really grab your reader.

The fifth paragraph will be on the second-third of your book. This is normally where a lot of the action and conflict happens. Remember, you don't want to give a lot of details and it doesn't have to be worded pretty, you just want to get the facts down.

The sixth paragraph will deal with the final third of your story – the resolution/conclusion. Here is where you see the story wrap itself up and answer all of the questions that readers may have, tie up all of the loose ends.

Any paragraphs written after that point should be dedicated to your secondary characters. Not much has to be written about them; they don't need a real history like your main characters but they do need some basic information written about them. Who are they? How are they related to the main characters (friend, nemesis, relative, neighbor, worst nightmare, etc)? You want to give them a physical description so that you won't forget. It's easy to overlook what a secondary character looks like when they aren't in every scene like your main ones so make sure that you know what they look like.

How are you doing so far? Are you overwhelmed? Wishing that you'd never signed up (or had your mom sign you up) for this workshop?

©2011 Stacey Cotrufo

It's challenging and again, time consuming but you are going to reap the rewards of knowing this information as you continue to write in the future.

Now that we have our detailed outline and can see where our story is going and what's going to happen and to whom, now we need to look at timelines and what the time range is for your book.

There is no right or wrong answer to this one. There is no formula or a rule. It's your story and it can happen as quickly as you want or over a span of months, years or decades; it's all up to you. The important thing to remember is to keep in time with your time line and what I mean by that is to make sure that your story, your characters, age along with the passage of time.

Back in the day (and I'm not proud of this) I used to watch soap operas. I was always annoyed with the fact that characters would get pregnant, have a baby three months later and then by the end of the summer that child was a toddler or going to school! The rest of the characters stayed the same. Time had passed normally for everyone except super-fetus who managed to come in to the world practically as an adult!

Keep in time with your timeline!!!

If your character is 15 at the beginning of your story, and the story takes place over a summer, the most they can be is 16 by the end of it and doing things that a 16 year old does. That means that they shouldn't be married, going to college or working on Wall Street. Those things just are not NORMAL for a 16 year old.

If your story takes place over a span of months, there isn't too much to think about, but if it is over years, and it's being written in modern/present time, then you need to pay attention to when your story starts and what inventions, technology, etc. are applicable. You don't want to be talking about the latest iPad if you decided to start your story in 2009.

©2011 Stacey Cotrufo

Introduction to Fiction Writing   Lesson Six – page 37

Draw an actual timeline. At the start of it, all the way over to the left, is where your story begins. What year? Underneath that, if you are so inclined, you can write what happens at that point in the story. Plot out what is going to happen and when.

This can be very basic – just you drawing a line and marking points in your story or you can get techy with it and go to a link like this one: http://www.wonderhowto.com/how-to-use-timeline-organize-flow-events-your-novel-408126/ or this one http://timeglider.com/
and see how to map this out on your computer. It's all up to you. They key, once again is to keep your story on a realistic track and it's easier to do that if you map it out with a timeline.

An example would be from a story that I was working on. In it the main characters have known each other for two years when the story first opens. From that first scene, the story will take place over the course of four months. There isn't much to know but I had to map it out in the sense that I didn't skip great chunks of time. If there was a scene where they were discussing an upcoming event that would happen in two weeks time, I made sure that I didn't just skip ahead to that event – I wrote a little bit of what happened in between events.

The seasons changed a bit over that four month time – we started at the end of August and the story ended in December so we were going to see different temperatures which led to different wardrobe choices, there is the glorious fall foliage to see in certain scenes and finally a little bit of snow. The story was set in present day North Carolina so I was true to the weather of the area.

Having that time line written up allowed me to keep track at certain plot points of how I needed to change the setting, the clothes, etc.

Whew! That's a lot of planning, isn't it?

Homework:

So in case you haven't guessed it yet, your homework assignment is to do all of that! You will submit your detailed outline but realistically, there is no way to submit that timeline; I'm just going to trust that you do it and believe me, you will thank me later.

©2011 Stacey Cotrufo

Introduction to Fiction Writing   Lesson Six – page 38

Please take your time and remember that writing this outline does not commit you to writing this story with those details. This is clearly a starting point.

If there is one bit of advice that I would give above all else it would be that the writing process never ends. You will forever want to edit what you have written. I have completed novels and years later I can pick them up and STILL find things that I want to change.

Don't let anxiety or fear of not knowing exactly what you want to happen hinder you. Write whatever your first instinct is if you hit a point in the story where you don't quite know what should happen next. There are no wrong answers! So relax and have fun with this.

Just a quick side note, the next two lessons really go hand in hand with this one and you will be taking the information from those lessons and adding to this homework assignment. So the more thorough you make this assignment, the easier the next two will be. PLUS, I would like to encourage you to do this assignment and save it as a file on your computer so that you can go back to it and add to it/edit it as needed.

_____

_____

_____

_____

_____

_____

_____

©2011 Stacey Cotrufo

©2011 Stacey Cotrufo

Introduction to Fiction Writing

Plot Development

This lesson is sort of a part two to lesson six.

Your plot is what your story is about. I saw this description that I thought you would find easy to relate to:

If an author writes, "The king died and then the queen died," there is no plot for a story. But by writing, "The king died and then the queen died of grief," the writer has provided a plot line for a story.

A plot is a causal sequence of events, the "why" for the things that happen in the story. The plot draws the reader into the character's lives and helps the reader understand the choices that the characters make.

You have developed your characters in a previous lesson, what are you going to do with them? What is their purpose in your story? Wiki answers had this to say about what is plot development:

Plot development is how a book progresses. You start with the beginning and see what the details are that lead to the climax. The climax is the part in the book that everything leads up to. For example if someone has to make a big decision the climax is their answer. Then you see the declining actions. How the book winds down and that is it.

All that to say that the plot is your story. You have to create a story that has a beginning, a middle and an end and that has a purpose. I've read stories that just pretty much talk about nothing. The whole story is just about the day to day life of the characters. There is no conflict, there is no climax, and the characters are just there.

That is completely boring.

Think about what your story is about. What is the major conflict in your story? Conflict, I know, can be a scary word. The conflict does not have to be some sort of epic battle or anything quite that dramatic. Conflict can be an internal thing – choosing to make the right decision; or it can be a disagreement among friends or family.

©2011 Stacey Cotrufo

Don't let the idea of conflict become an obstacle for you; conflict is something that we deal with each and every day. Whether you are trying to decide whether or not to get up or stay in bed. Conflict. Do you do your school work or chores now or later? Conflict. Do you do the things that need to be done or do you procrastinate? Conflict. See? Even the simplest things that we do every day are sources of conflict.

You have your outline done from lesson six. And again, remember that it is not written in stone so you are not locked in to that particular story BUT we are going to take another look at that outline and really get a feel for your story.

You may have a story that deals with a character who meets somebody and they do not get along at all. They need to, for whatever the reason, but they have reasons why they seem to keep butting heads with one another. This is the basis of a lot of stories that have been written and it's a great premise but you have to decide what you are going to do differently to make your story stand out. What situations are you going to put them in to either make them fight to the finish or have them realize that they are not so different after all?

You have to develop that story. You have to look at what sort of things you want to see happen in the story, the places and people you want to incorporate in to the story itself and breathe life in to your words.

Developing your plot is an ongoing process that will keep you going until long after you've written the last page; it will continue will in to the editing process and possibly in to the publishing process. I don't say that to scare you, I say it to give you a realistic view of your writing so that you don't think "Well, I've just written 'The End' so I'm done."

Today's lesson is relatively short because I am going to refer you to some websites on the topic that can describe all of this far better than I am. I want you to consider this lesson to purely be research for the sake of your position as an author/writer. We always need to learn more about our craft. There are very few writers that know everything and can sit down and push out a book with very little effort. The more you know, however, the easier the process can be.

©2011 Stacey Cotrufo

Introduction to Fiction Writing — Lesson Seven

Homework:

I want you to visit the following three websites and read what they have to say. Then, as an additional little mini-assignment, I would like you write a short journal entry about your thoughts on the whole process – what do you think is challenging about it, do you feel comfortable with the process or overwhelmed? Give us a little insight in to how you are feeling at this stage of the workshop as a writer.

http://leigh-ann-andersen.suite101.com/writing-a-novel--developing-a-plot-a383349

http://www.ehow.com/how_2057344_develop-plot-fiction.html

http://www.thefreelibrary.com/Book+Writing+How+to+Develop+the+Plot+and+Characters+for+Your+Book-a01073978986

_____

_____

_____

_____

_____

_____

_____

_____

_____

©2011 Stacey Cotrufo

Conflict and Resolution

We touched upon the concept of conflict briefly in lesson seven so we're not going to spend too much time on it today.

As we talked about previously, there needs to be some sort of conflict in your story. Wiki Answers had this to say about conflict and resolution:

All literature is about conflict between two forces, the protagonist (the hero, the good guy) and the antagonist or antagonists (the villains or bad guys). Sometimes the antagonist isn't a person: it can be fate, the universe, God, the Devil. The antagonist can even be the protagonist (in a story where the conflict is between man and himself). But whoever or whatever the antagonist is, he/it is there to cause a problem for the protagonist. This problem, and the solving of it, is the story.

You wouldn't want to read a story where there is no conflict to resolve. It's boring. Who wants to read a story about a character just going about their daily life, waking up, going to work, coming home, watching TV, etc. That's not a story; that's just a written account of someone's existence.

What makes a story interesting -- what makes a story a story, in fact -- is that early on in the story, the protagonist is presented with a problem, a conflict between himself and an opposing force, and he spends the rest of the story trying to solve it. In essence, that is all a story is: setting up a conflict, and having your lead character or characters resolve it.

Typically, the first half of the story is about setting up the conflict between the two people or forces (the protagonist and antagonist), and the second half of the story is about resolving that conflict. That's what conflict resolution is: how the author, through the characters, solves the problem and ends the conflict.

Thinking about your story, what is your source of conflict? What is happening between your characters to create that conflict? How are you, as the writer, going to keep that antagonism going throughout the story?

©2011 Stacey Cotrufo

But more importantly, how are you going to resolve it? In most cases, you do not want to leave the reader hanging, unless your book is one in a series and even then there has to be some resolution at the end of the book.

I always get angry when I am watching a TV show that I have invested and hour's worth of my time in to, to only have it say "To Be Continued" at the end of it. In literature, you don't want to have a "To Be Continued" option. You need to have an ending, a resolution at the end of your book.

I am currently reading book three in a trilogy. The books are all set in the same town but each book has its own main characters. The secondary characters are the same and we see them in each book and learn a little more about them, but each book focuses on one main story.

This series dealt with triplet sisters. Each book was dedicated and focused on each individual sister and what was going on in her life. The author still mentioned the other triplets in each book, but each sister got her own story. You can HINT at another story that would sort of be a continuation of the book you are writing, but you want to finish the story you are writing and give your reader something to look forward to, not make them angry that they are left with answers.

For the sake of this workshop, let's assume that you are writing a single-title book. It's not part of a series, there is no part two, no to be continued. You are going to have a story that has a definite beginning, middle and an end.

Again, this all is part of the plot outline process. You need to consider all of that as we go along. That is just one of the reasons that I told you to not think of the outline as something that is written in stone. It will be changing for a long time. I know that the process may seem a little out of order – after all, I had you write the outline already and now we keep going back in to the story to add more details!

©2011 Stacey Cotrufo

Introduction to Fiction Writing   Lesson Eight – page 46

Think about the outline as a process within itself. You had the skeleton outline, then you had a more detailed outline, soon you will have enough information that you will have the most thorough outline so that you can begin your book and have possibly an eighth to a quarter of the book done just in the outline! That is a huge amount to have written before you've even started the book!

Again, this lesson is short because each of you is working on a different story. I would like for you to think about your conflict in your story and how you are going to resolve it. What is the turning point in your story where your character redeems himself or where enemies become friends or where you get to the happily ever after?

Homework:

I want you to sum up your story's conflict in one paragraph of up to ten sentences. Then I would like you to, in a separate paragraph write up how you plan to resolve that conflict. I would like you to include as many details as possible at this stage of your planning. The resolution needs to tie up all loose ends and storylines/sub plots so be sure to include them.

_____

_____

_____

_____

_____

_____

_____

©2011 Stacey Cotrufo

Dialogue

I normally dedicate an entire workshop (4 weeks) to this topic but we are going to condense it down as much as possible to give you the basics of dialogue writing today. Okay, so let's take a 4-week class and condense it down to the basics. Ready?

Dialogue is an important part of any fiction story. In most cases you have more than one character in your story and at some point, they are going to have to communicate. For the sake of today's lesson, we are going to keep our dialogue between only two people.

The key to good dialogue writing is good listening. Take some time to observe how the people around you speak. What do they sound like, what are their facial expressions and what kind of gestures do they make while talking. People can be very animated when they speak and if you want to write some great dialogue that readers can relate to, spend some time observing the people around you and even yourself!

If you listen to conversations around you or really think about a conversation that you have had with someone, you will see that we do not use proper English all of the time, so why would your characters? We are not perfect and so chances are that our characters aren't going to be, either. It's okay to use slang and fragments – just not all the time.

Remember the basic structure of writing dialogue: Always use quotation marks around a quote that someone is saying, always capitalize the first letter of the work in the quotation and make sure that you use proper punctuation (question marks, commas, etc) within the quotation. If anyone has more questions on this part, please let me know and I have a supplemental lesson to help.

Make sure that you separate who is speaking when you are writing. What I mean by that is that a new paragraph is started whenever you change speakers. You do not want to have two people (or more) speaking within the same paragraph. It MUST be separated.

©2011 Stacey Cotrufo

Introduction to Fiction Writing   Lesson Nine – page 50

You have a thorough description of your characters. You know how you want them to sound and speak. Make sure that you stay on task with that whenever you have them speak. If your character is a child, then they are not going to be using large words. If your character is uneducated, they will probably speak with more slang words and if your character is well-educated, they must speak that way. You want their personalities to come through in their dialogue so be sure that you are familiar with the people you created.

Where is this dialogue taking place? If your scene is set in a church, the dialogue would be very different than if it were going on in a stadium. You need to convey that in HOW your characters speak. I like to think of this as reminding you that not everything is "Said". What I mean by that is that we often just add "He said" or "She said" at the end of a sentence of dialogue but really, is everything always just "said"?

We laugh, we joke, we whisper, we scream, we have emotions when we speak. Remember that when you are writing! The reader doesn't know what is in your head so if you don't convey to your reader HOW your characters are feeling and how they are saying something, it can hamper how they view your scene.

Someone who is depressed in a scene needs to be written in a way that describes that – particularly if you are only going by dialogue. This is what I mainly want to focus on today. Because dialogue is so important, you need to know when and how to use it. If your whole book was dialogue, it would be tedious. If there was no dialogue, it would be boring.

I recently read a book where the whole story was told via e-mail interactions between a few different people. I hated it. There was no emotion, no setting…it was crazy boring. How are we, the reader, supposed to know what is going on in a character's mind or how something was meant if there is no indication of it from the writer. Think about how you write an email. You don't include a narration with it so that form of writing is really not appropriate for a novel or short story.

©2011 Stacey Cotrufo

My final thought on dialogue is this: Do not over do it. This is a quote that I found from a website geared toward authors:

I think dialogue is incredibly hard to write -- and very hard to write well. Trying to make it read like a conversation, not an info dump, not loading it with tons of dialogue tags which add weight but no meaning, making it a scene that leads to action or carries action. Or using it as an external reveal for the character speaking to make his or her thoughts a public, rather than a private realization, to the reader and the other characters in the scene is difficult to pull off not just once, but throughout the whole of the book. Yes, all the balance of the rest of those elements -- setting, scene, action, internal and external conflict -- make a good book, but amazing dialogue makes a good book a great one.

Your dialogue is meant to add another layer to your story. You can narrate a story all day long but the addition of good dialogue will help your readers connect to your characters. You want their voices to come through loud and clear. However, if you take that dialogue and weigh it down with a lot of "he said/she said" or describe the way that each and every quote was said, it gets to be too much.

If your dialogue between two characters is going on, you should not have to put who is speaking and how after each sentence they speak. Space it out, find other ways of writing so that your reader does not find you repeating yourself.

This lesson frustrates me because there is so much more that we can do with this but I'm limited due to the length of the book. I know that we basically just skimmed the surface and if you have any questions, please feel free to ask because there is so much more to be said on this subject, you can refer to the other workbook in the series, "The Art of Dialogue Writing." It's currently available in this same format and can give you a lot more in-depth instructions on how to master this topic.

©Stacey Cotrufo

Homework:

This assignment is going to have three parts but I think you will be able to handle it just fine. The first part: I want you to create a scene for your characters, one where there is no dialogue and it is just you describing their actions/what they are doing.

For the second part, I want you to take that same scene and interject some dialogue between the two of them. Basically you will use all of your describing and your writing from part one and just add some dialogue to it.

In the final part I want you to simply use dialogue to tell the whole scene. You are going to simplify the descriptions and let the characters tell what is going on by what they are saying to one another.

_____

_____

_____

_____

_____

_____

_____

_____

_____

_____

©2011 Stacey Cotrufo

Paragraph and Chapter Structure

At this point in your lives, you've written paragraphs. You may not think about them much while you are writing them, but in your school assignments or in your emails your style of writing will probably lean towards writing in paragraphs.

In everything you read, you'll find that it is divided in to paragraph form. If a book or story were written as one big long paragraph, it would be chaos. You need to break up your story in to paragraphs for the reader to understand what is going on, to identify dialogue, to set the scene, to direct the story, etc. Again, if you've written any kind of book report or essay, the concept of paragraphs should be a given, but just in case you are unsure, we'll hit the basic rules:

What is a paragraph?

A paragraph is a collection of related sentences dealing with a single topic. Learning to write good paragraphs will help you as a writer stay on track during your drafting and revision stages. Good paragraphing also greatly assists your readers in following a piece of writing. You can have fantastic ideas, but if those ideas aren't presented in an organized fashion, you will lose your readers (and fail to achieve your goals in writing).

The Basic Rule: Keep One Idea to One Paragraph

The basic rule of thumb with paragraphing is to keep one idea to one paragraph. If you begin to transition into a new idea, it belongs in a new paragraph. There are some simple ways to tell if you are on the same topic or a new one. You can have one idea and several bits of supporting evidence within a single paragraph. You can also have several points in a single paragraph as long as they relate to the overall topic of the paragraph. If the single points start to get long, then perhaps elaborating on each of them and placing them in their own paragraphs is the route to go.

©2011 Stacey Cotrufo

How do I know when to start a new paragraph?

You should start a new paragraph when:

- **When you begin a new idea or point.** New ideas should always start in new paragraphs. If you have an extended idea that spans multiple paragraphs, each new point within that idea should have its own paragraph.
- **To contrast information or ideas.** Separate paragraphs can serve to contrast sides in a debate, different points in an argument, or any other difference.
- **When your readers need a pause.** Breaks in paragraphs function as a short "break" for your readers—adding these in will help your writing more readable. You would create a break if the paragraph becomes too long or the material is complex.
- **When you are ending your introduction or starting your conclusion.** Your introductory and concluding material should always be in a new paragraph. Many introductions and conclusions have multiple paragraphs depending on their content, length, and the writer's purpose.

Okay, so that is the basics on writing a paragraph. Remember to keep your paragraphs on topic and don't make them too long and you'll have happy readers. The next type of paragraph we'll look at have to do with dialogue writing. I know I didn't go in to too much detail with that in the previous lesson but that was because I knew we'd handle it here.

These are the basic rules for writing dialogue within your story:

Always use quotation marks to begin and end a direct quotation.
Use a comma to separate who is speaking from what is being said.

James said, "I won't be able to make it to the movies tonight." OR
"I won't be able to make it to the movies tonight," James said.

©2011 Stacey Cotrufo

If a question mark or exclamation point occurs where one of the separating commas should be, delete the comma and use the question mark or exclamation point to separate the material.

"I won't be able to make it to the movies tonight!" James yelled.

Always capitalize the first word in the quotation.

*He said, "**W**e'll find another time to go and hang out."*

If you divide your quotation in half by interjecting who is speaking, use a capital letter to start the sentence but you do not capitalize again until a new sentence starts.

"I won't be able to make it to the movies tonight," James said, "because I have to go to work."

"I won't be able to make it to the movies tonight," James sighed. "My boss called me in to work."

*See the difference between those two examples? In the first one, I put who was speaking in the middle of the quote whereas in the second one, I put who was speaking between two separate sentences.

Periods and commas ALWAYS go INSIDE the quotation marks.

"I wish I was on vacation right now," Nick said.

Nick said, "I wish I was on vacation right now.

©Stacey Cotrufo

When you write dialogue, always begin a new paragraph whenever the speaker changes.

"I'd say we are more than done, Mr. Lawrence." She was proud of the fact that her voice sounded steady and that she had her temper under control. "CJ's has enjoyed providing our service for all of your events for the last two years but this is one time that I simply cannot meet your request. It's unreasonable of you to ask that we change the entire menu on such short notice. If you'd like to find another event planner and caterer that is your prerogative."

"I don't want another event planner, Cassandra," Adam replied irritably. "We have a contract; one that states that changes can be made…"

"Up to two weeks before," she cut in with frustration.

"The L.S.S. Fall Retreat is two weeks away," he replied mildly, clearly believing to have the upper hand. His confidence tipped a bit when he noticed Cassie had her own triumphant smile as she reached in to her leather brief case.

Pulling out her day planner, Cassie opened to September's calendar and turned it to face Adam. "Today is the twelfth; your retreat is on the twenty-third. That is eleven days, not two weeks."

Use a series of three dots (Ellipsis Points) to indicate an abrupt break in thought or speech or an unfinished statement or question.

"First of all," he said, "we have a contract, Cassandra, and it clearly states that I have the option of changing the menu. If you'll recall…"

"Changes can be made up to two weeks before," she cut in with frustration.

"…and the L.S.S. Fall Retreat is only two weeks away!" Adam finished, equally frustrated.

*In some grammar books, you will be told to use an em dash (which is a series of two dashes) but I prefer the three dots method.

©Stacey Cotrufo

If you have the same person (character) saying lengthy dialogue, you may choose to keep everything in one paragraph or separate parts in to their own paragraphs. Make this decision using the same criteria you would use in deciding to start a new paragraph without dialogue in it. Meaning, if your character is talking about several different topics, give each one their own paragraph. Always make sure, however, that you make it clear who is speaking at all times.

AND

When a speaker's words run for more than one paragraph, use quotation marks at the beginning of the quotation, at the beginning of each paragraph, and at the end of the whole quotation.

    "I don't see how you can expect me to make these changes on such short notice, Mr. Lawrence," Cassie said. "We had an agreement. I have organized this event based on that agreement and asking me to change that at this point would create a lot of extra work for me!"
    "Besides that, we have a legally binding contract. You are asking me to break the contract when in fact it is you, sir, who is breaking it."
    "I hardly see where that is the case," he said.
    "Trust me, I've been dealing with this sort of thing for years and what you are doing is breaking the contract by asking me to make these changes. If you'd like to ask your lawyer...?"
    "That won't be necessary, Cassandra," Adam said quietly, "we'll continue with things as they are."

Okay, I know that there was a lot of information there but for the most part, this is all stuff that you probably have learned in your English and Language Art lessons over the years. Don't let dialogue writing scare you; just remember how to separate it within your story and to keep it clear as to who is speaking at all times.

©Stacey Cotrufo

Chapters are a little more tricky and really, how long or how short you want them depends on your style of writing and what it is that you are trying to convey. For example, I know a lot of writers make their chapters very short – maybe five or six pages each. Their stories are fast paced and can pull off a short chapter format. Other stories, other novels require a meatier chapter – anywhere from fifteen to thirty pages.

What I'm saying is that there is no magical number. Every story is different and so where and how you divide it up is completely up to you. However, you want the chapter breaks to make sense.

For example, you would not end a chapter in the middle of a sentence. That's obvious, right? BUT you can end a chapter in the middle of a scene. Sometimes it's good to end a chapter at a point where it's almost like a cliffhanger…you know, a "To Be Continued" or something like that.

The best way for you to figure out how you want your chapters formatted is to read the kind of books that you enjoy reading and that you find yourself writing like and see how they do it. Again, no secret answers, no magical recipe to make it work – you, as the author, get to pick how you want to make it all work out.

Homework:

I know there was a lot of reading in this and a lot of rules to take in to consideration so I will keep the assignment fairly simple. I would like you to write a couple of paragraphs from your story. Give me some samples of dialogue within your paragraphs, some scene setting and a glimpse in to what your story is about. Make it 3-5 paragraphs and remember that they usually tend to be anywhere from 4-10 sentences each.

©Stacey Cotrufo

The Art of Dialogue Writing

Avoiding Stereotypes & Clichés

Definition: A stereotype is a character, with generalized traits (characteristics that make the character a group representative rather than an individual). Writers sometimes use stereotypes as minor characters.

A **stereotype** is a popular belief about specific social groups or types of individuals. The concepts of "stereotype" and "prejudice" are often confused with many other different meanings. Stereotypes are standardized and simplified conceptions of groups based on some prior assumptions.

The definition of a **stereotype** is any commonly known public belief about a certain social group or a type of individual. Stereotypes are often confused with prejudices, because, like prejudices, a stereotype is based on a prior assumption. Stereotypes are often created about people of specific cultures or races.

Okay, having stated a sampling of definitions for stereotype let me say this: Not all stereotypes are bad...BUT...sometimes they are overused and have the potential to be offensive. Some of the more obvious stereotypes are that blonde's are less intelligent than brunettes, all Italians have mafia connections, all New Yorkers are rude, all Southerners are rednecks...I'm sure you've heard your share of things like this.

Don't lock your characters in to such obvious stereotypes. Readers don't enjoy it and it can really show a lack of creativity or hinder your creativity. You are creating people who can be anything that you want them to be so make them individuals; make them people that readers aren't so familiar with that they have no desire to read about them. Make them YOURS. Don't let someone else's description, idea or whatever change what you have in mind for your characters.

Now what about clichés? Let's see...how do we describe a cliché? A **cliché** is an expression, idea, or element of an artistic work which has been overused to the point of losing its original meaning or effect, rendering it a stereotype, especially when at some earlier time it was considered meaningful or novel. Most phrases now considered clichéd were originally regarded as striking, but lost their force through overuse.

©2011 Stacey Cotrufo

Definition of *CLICHÉ (from Websters)*

1: a trite phrase or expression; *also* : the idea expressed by it
2: a hackneyed theme, characterization, or situation
3: something (as a menu item) that has become overly familiar or commonplace

This topic is so much fun for me because as I was researching it, I found so many websites that listed different types of clichés in books and movies that I found myself laughing out loud. Here are some examples of clichés from movies. Think about how many times you've seen these things and how often you've yelled at the screen because it's ridiculous:

Whenever anyone is chased to a staircase, s/he will run upstairs rather than down

Characters who survive a plane crash onto a desert island can go for weeks without bathing, get dragged through mud pits, battle with local wildlife and still come out with their hair and clothing looking professionally styled.

At least one of a pair of identical twins is born evil.

People never cough, sneeze, blow their noses, or show any other symptoms of being in less than perfect health. Only exception to the this is when they're dying. A cough is a symptom of terminal illness.

Bombs always have big, blinking, beeping timer displays. Evil geniuses who devise bombs to destroy things/people are always thoughtful enough to include a visible display (usually LED) of how much time remains before the bomb detonates, giving the hero accurate feedback on exactly how much time remains.

There are always people carrying around large sheets of glass on the street during a car chase.

©2011 Stacey Cotrufo

People being chased by a car will keep running down the middle of the road instead of ducking in somewhere where a car cannot go.

People who hear something weird outside will go OUT to look, even if they know there's a homicidal maniac on the loose.

A malfunctioning or burnt light bulb usually means that someone is hiding in the room, ready to jump on our hero/heroine while he/she's busy hitting the switch or tapping the bulb.

More often than not, the best method to revive somebody after their heart has stopped, assuming that there has already been a lengthy attempt to revive them with CPR, those electric zapper things, ect. is screaming at them something like:
"You never backed away from everything in your life, now fight! Fight! FIIIGHT!" or
"You can't do this to me! I love you, dammit!"

For more of these observations, you can go to:
http://www.moviecliches.com/cliche2.html#elevators

Another form of clichés comes in form of phrases. Some examples that most people are familiar with include:

ace in the hole
back against the wall
back in the saddle
back to square one
back to the drawing board
bad to the bone
badge of honor
bored to tears
born and raised
born with a silver spoon in your mouth
bored to tears
born and raised
born with a silver spoon in your mouth

©2011 Stacey Cotrufo

calm before the storm
darkest before the dawn
dead as a doornail
every dog has its day

There are a TON of these out there and to see a more complete list, go to: http://suspense.net/whitefish/cliche.htm

In the end, the goal is to make you aware of these things so that you do not fill your stories with these phrases and scenes so that no reader will be rolling their eyes at you. Classic movie lines are great…in those movies. Using some of those classic lines (particularly the ones at the end of a movie) tends to annoy readers. They are looking for something fresh; they are looking for something original that they haven't read before.

BE THAT AUTHOR! WRITE THAT SCENE! END THAT BOOK IN AN ORIGINAL WAY!

Not everyone "lives happily every after". There isn't always a "calm before the storm". Sometimes there is chaos; sometimes relationships end. Not every woman who has ever been proposed to has answered with "Yes, yes… a thousand times, yes!"

Homework:

So this is our very last assignment and I want you to do a couple of things. First, I'd like you to list your top five most annoying clichés (words, phrases or movie scenes). Next, I'd like you to pick a clichéd line from a movie (or book) that you would NOT use to end your story.

Then, for one last challenge, I'd like you to write a scene that is FULL of stereotypes and clichés – it doesn't have to be based on your actual story, it can be just a random scene.

©2011 Stacey Cotrufo

The Art of Dialogue Writing   Lesson One – page 68

Made in the USA
San Bernardino, CA
13 April 2017